Machines That Go

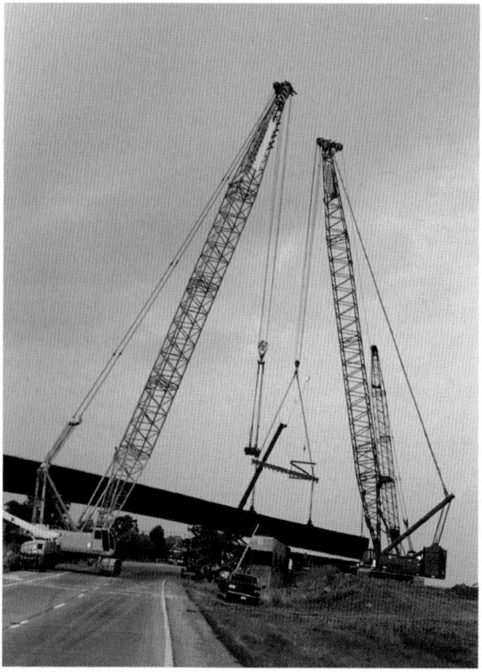

written by Pam Holden

C is for car.

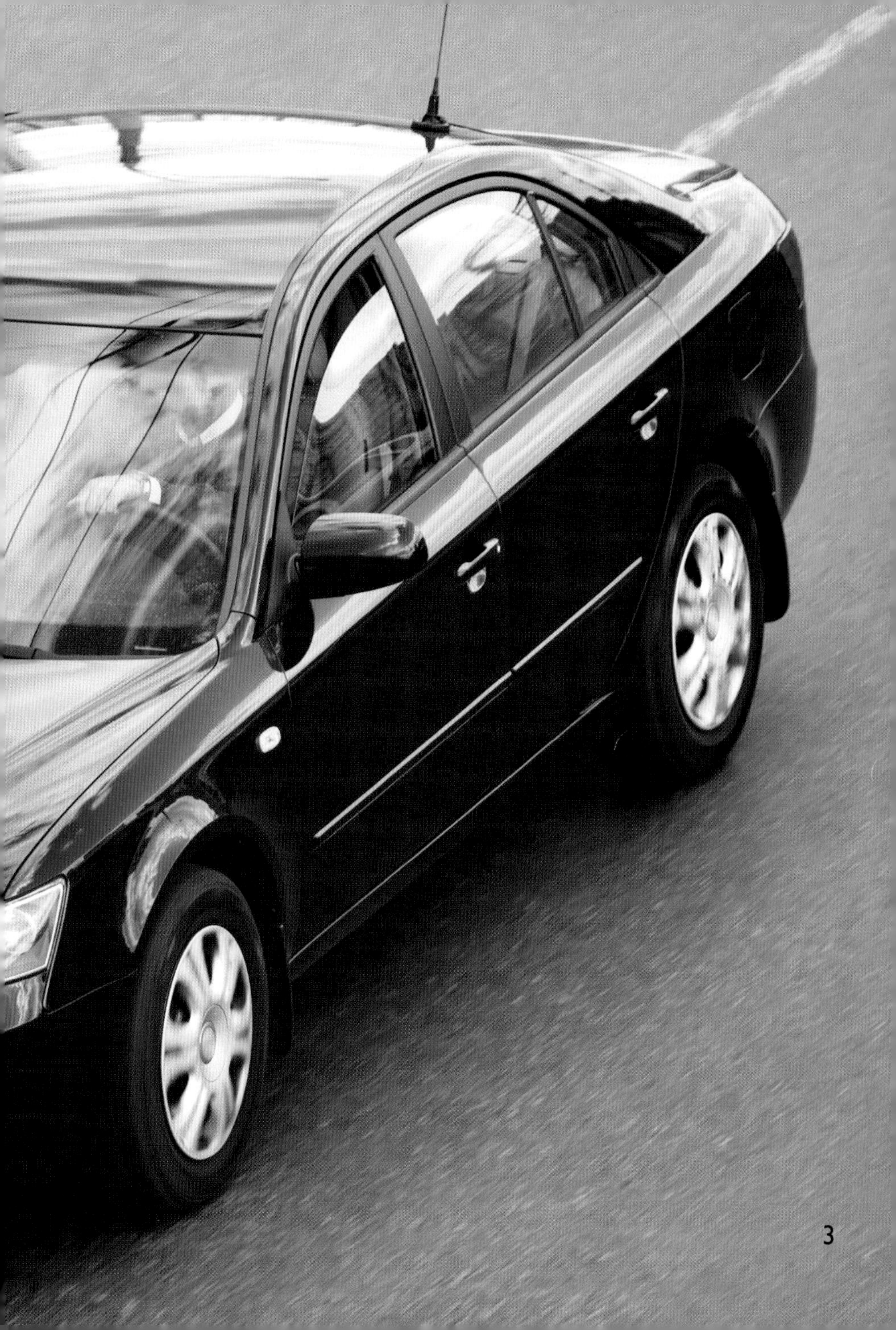

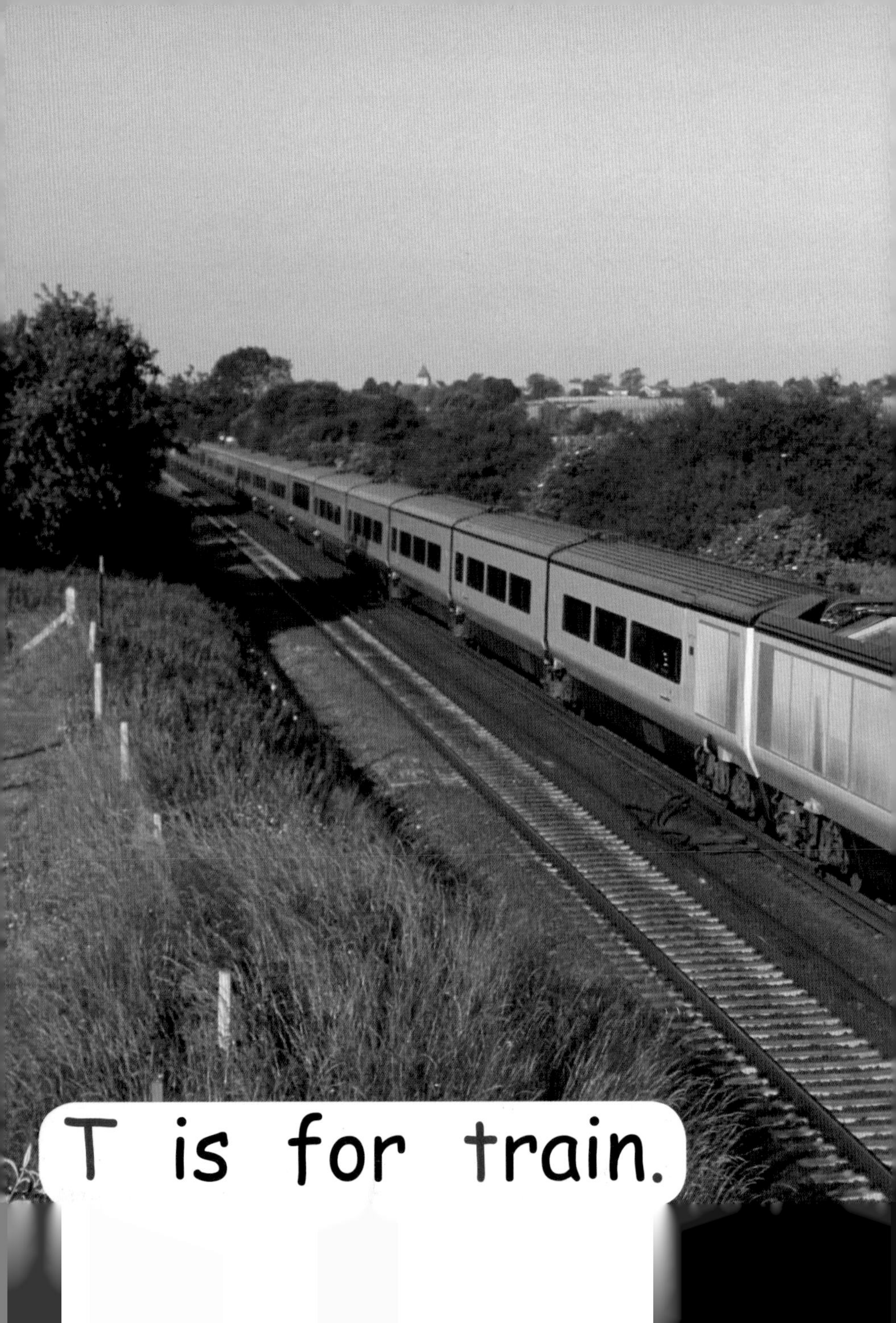

T is for train.

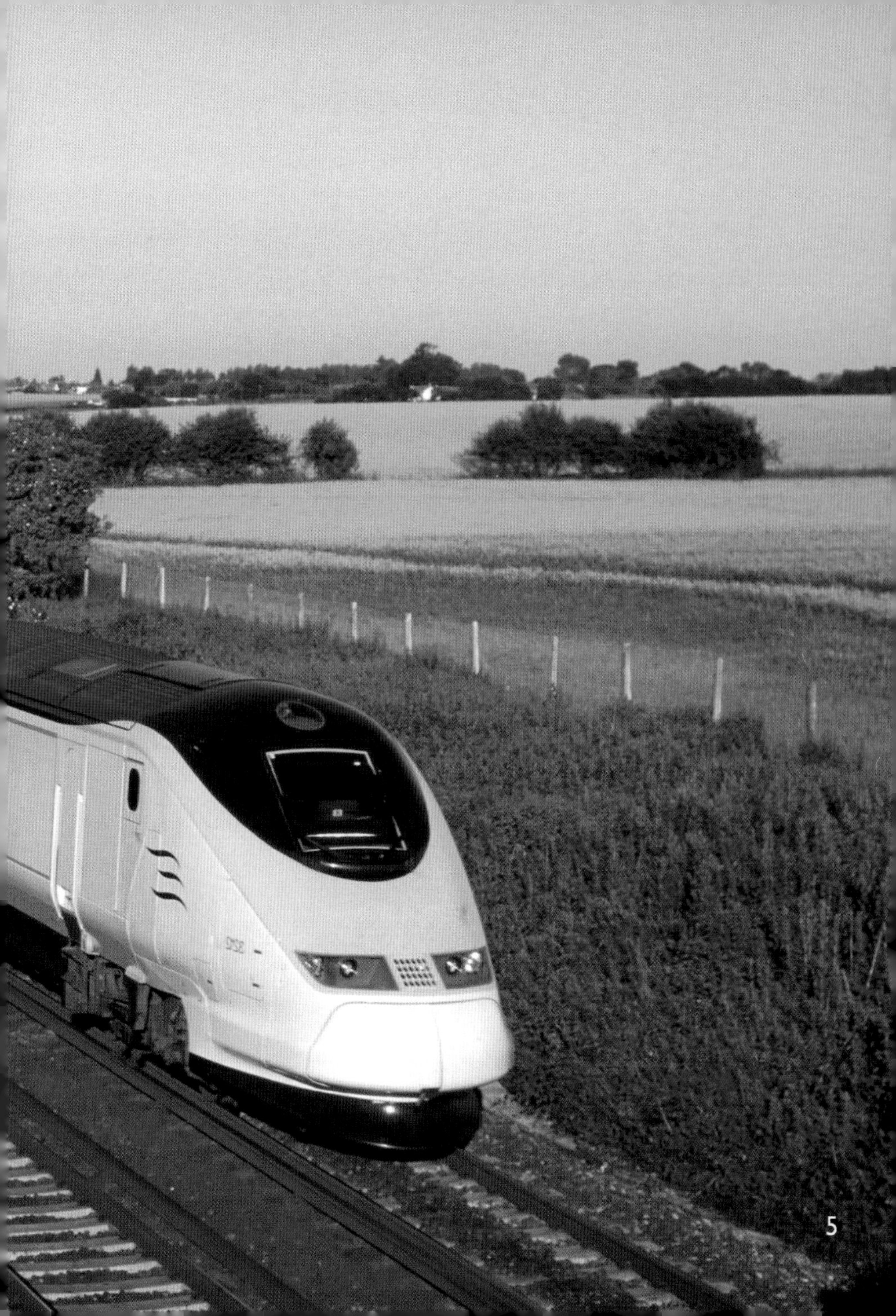

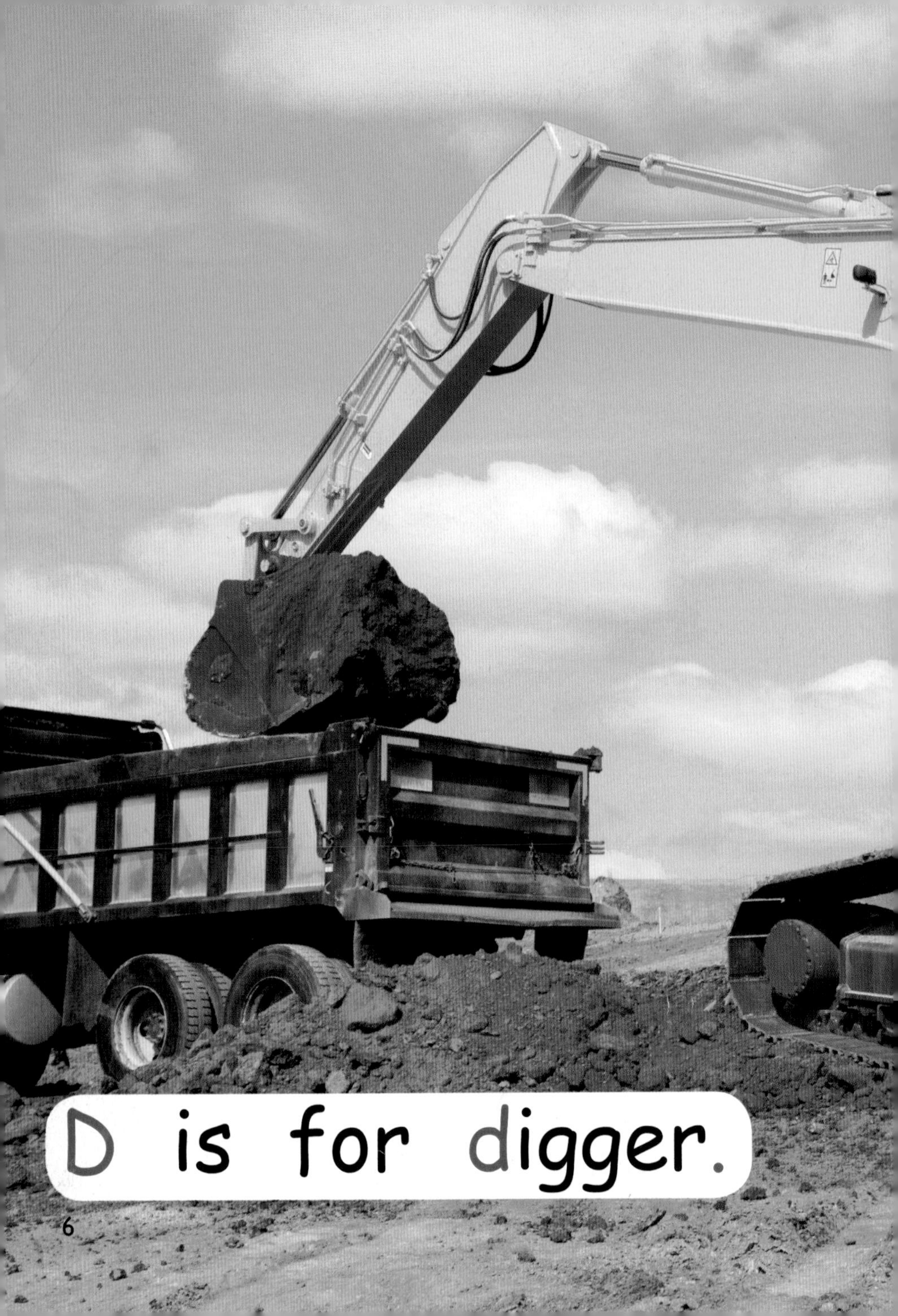

D is for digger.

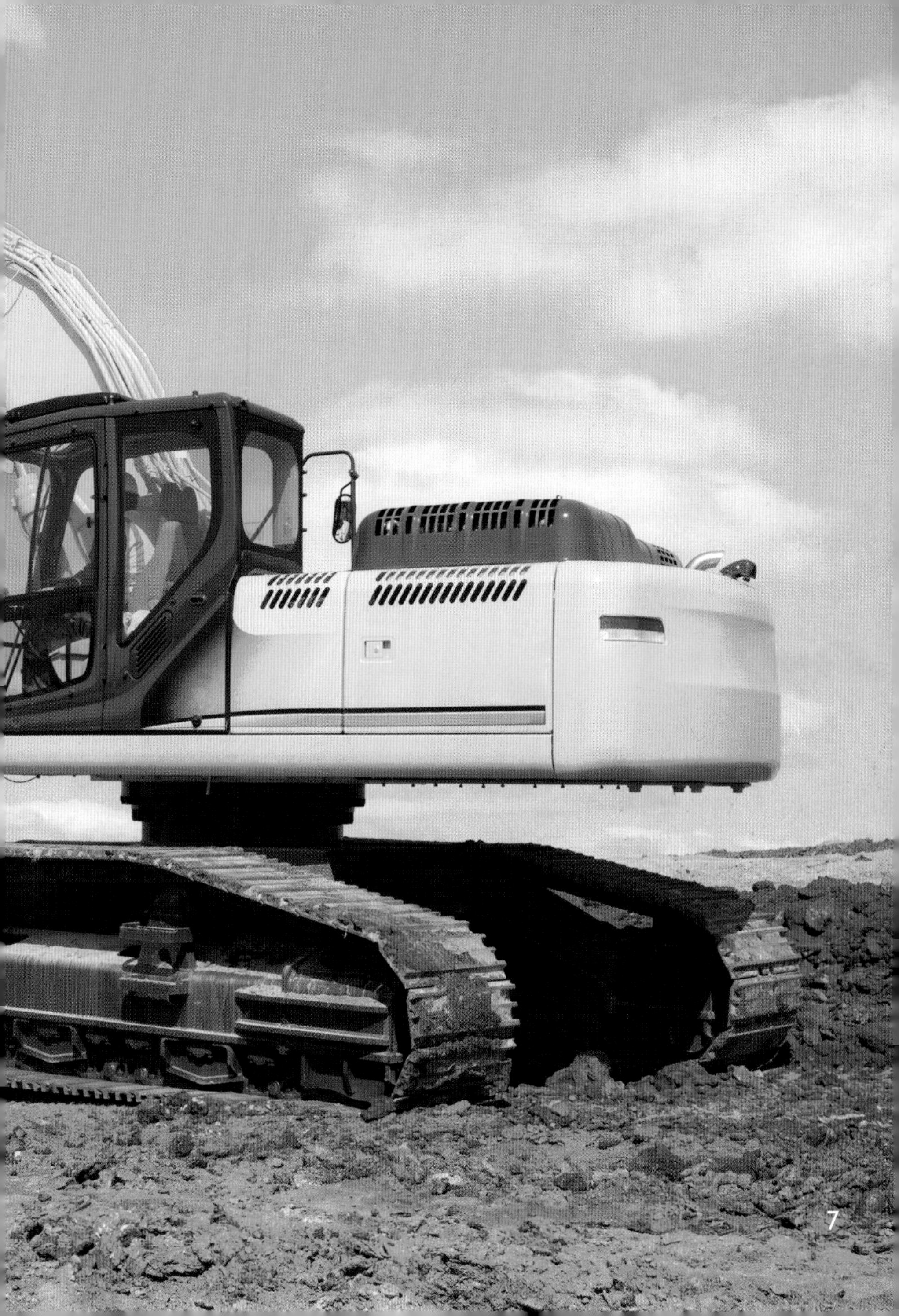

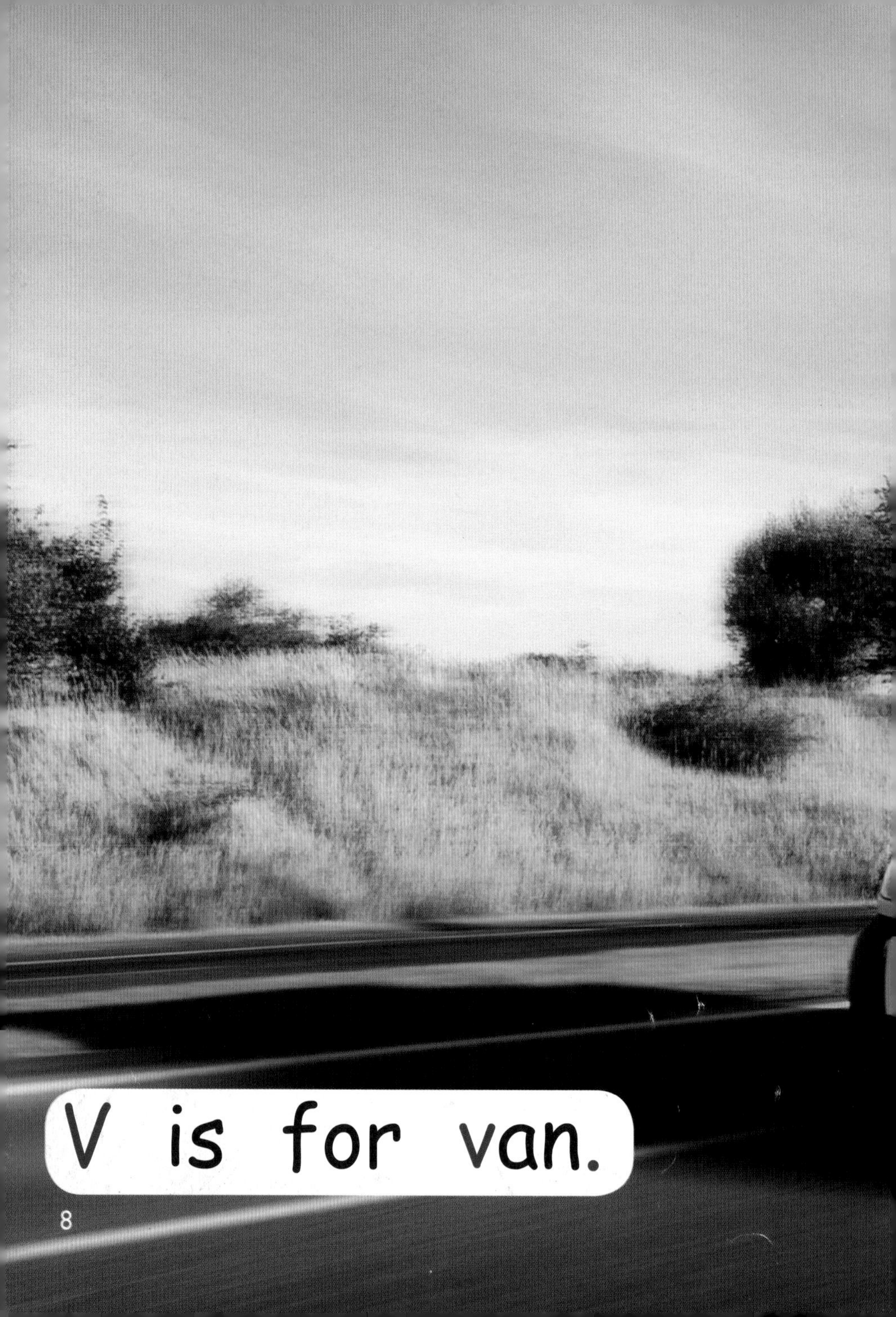

V is for van.

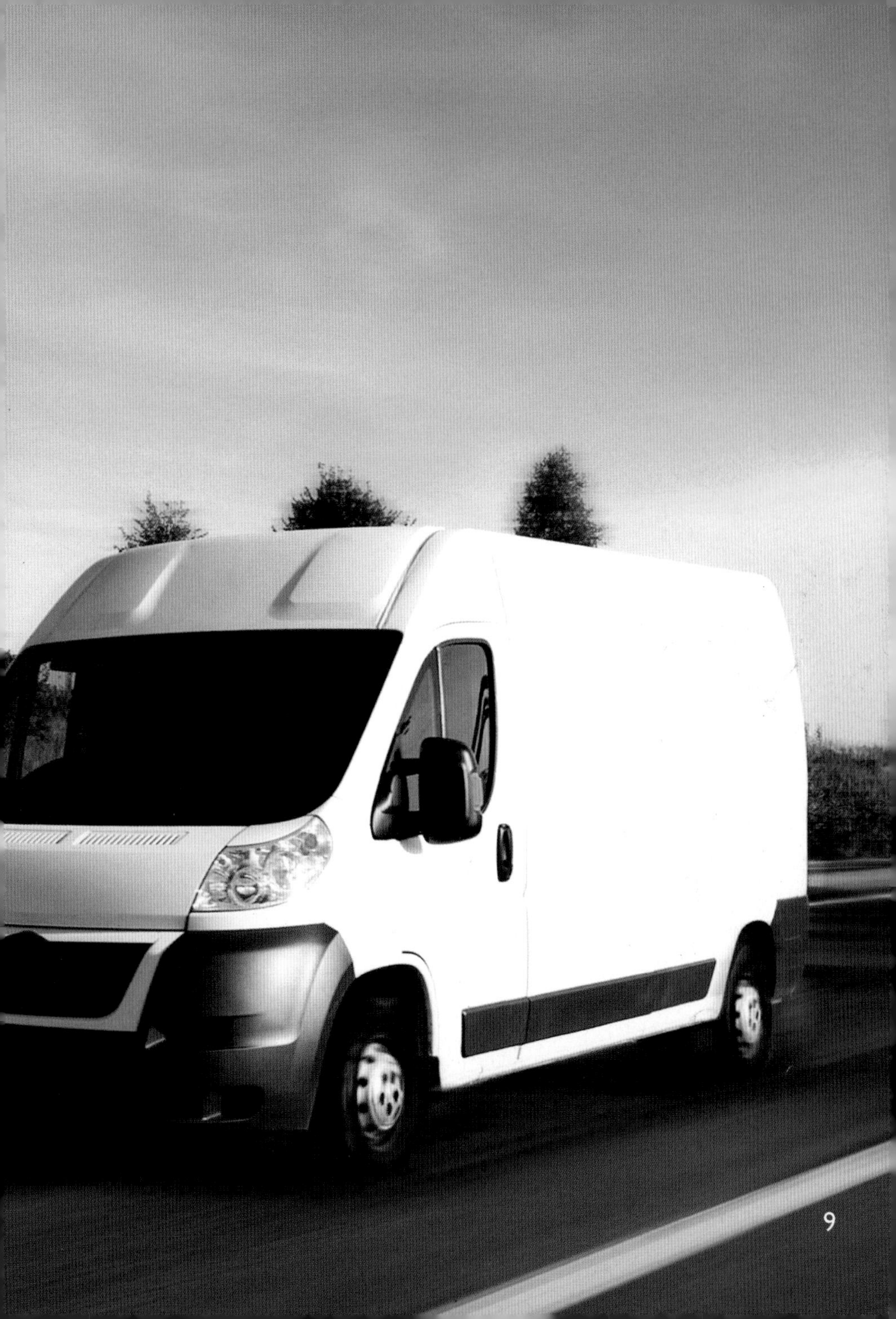

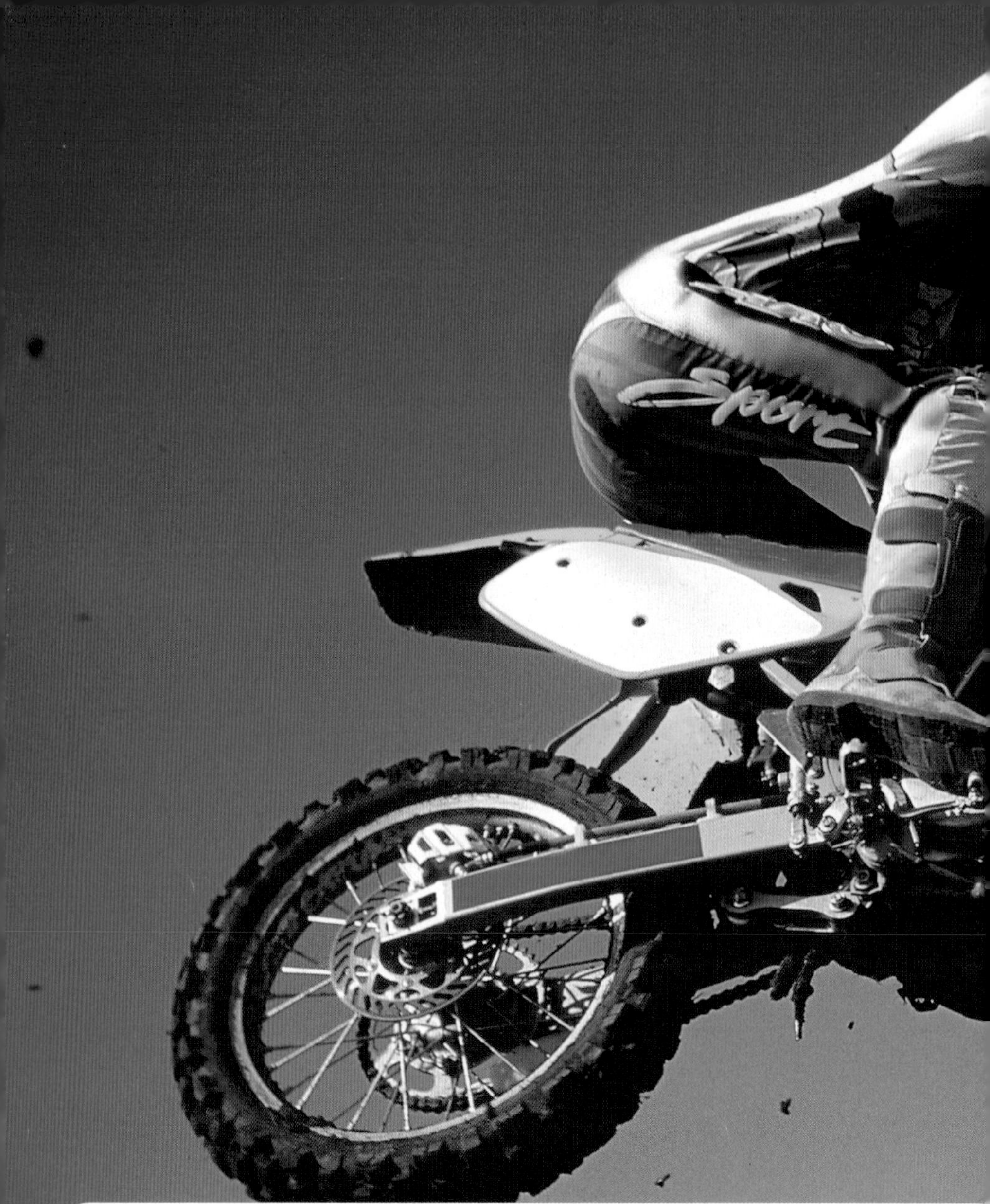

M is for motorcycle

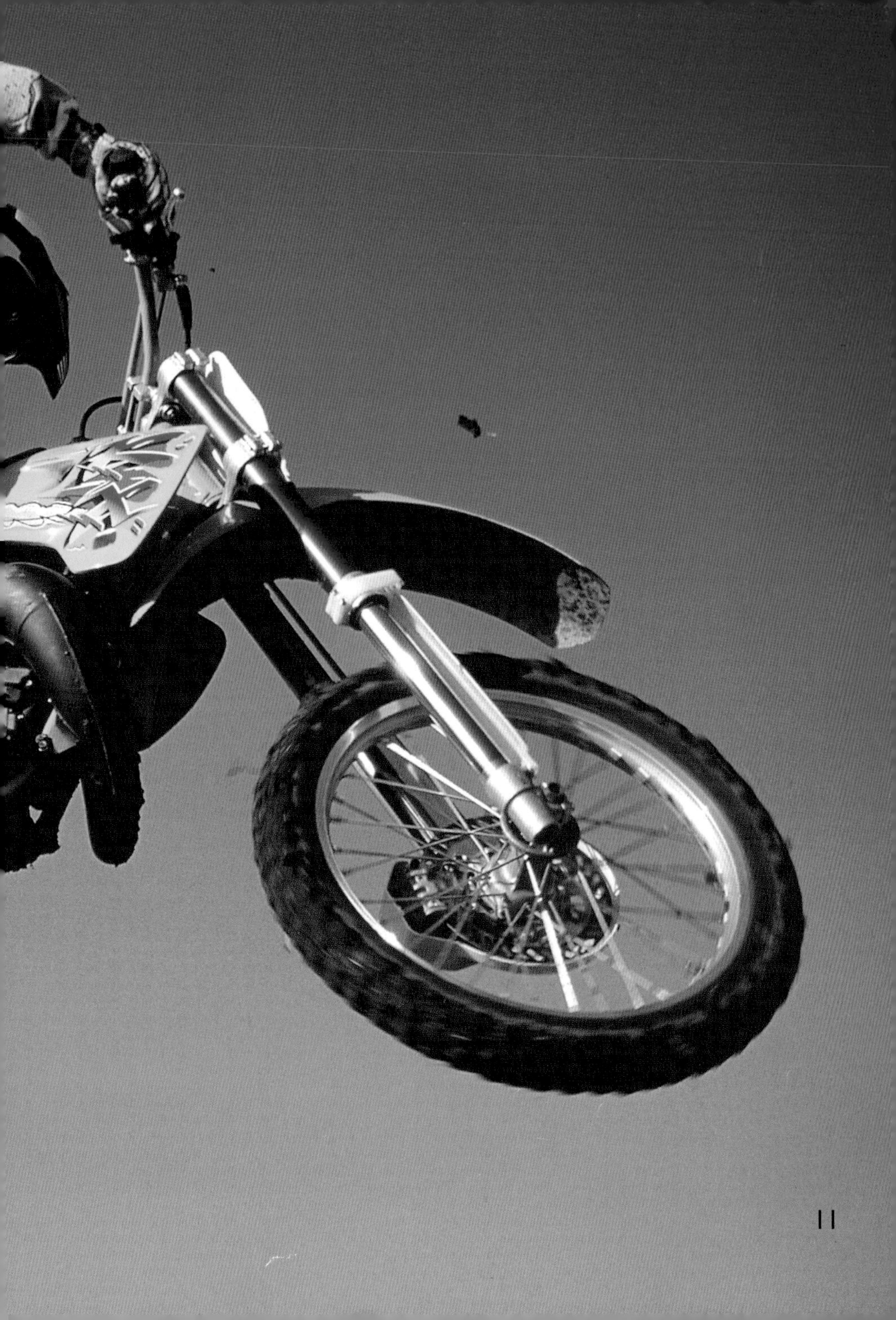

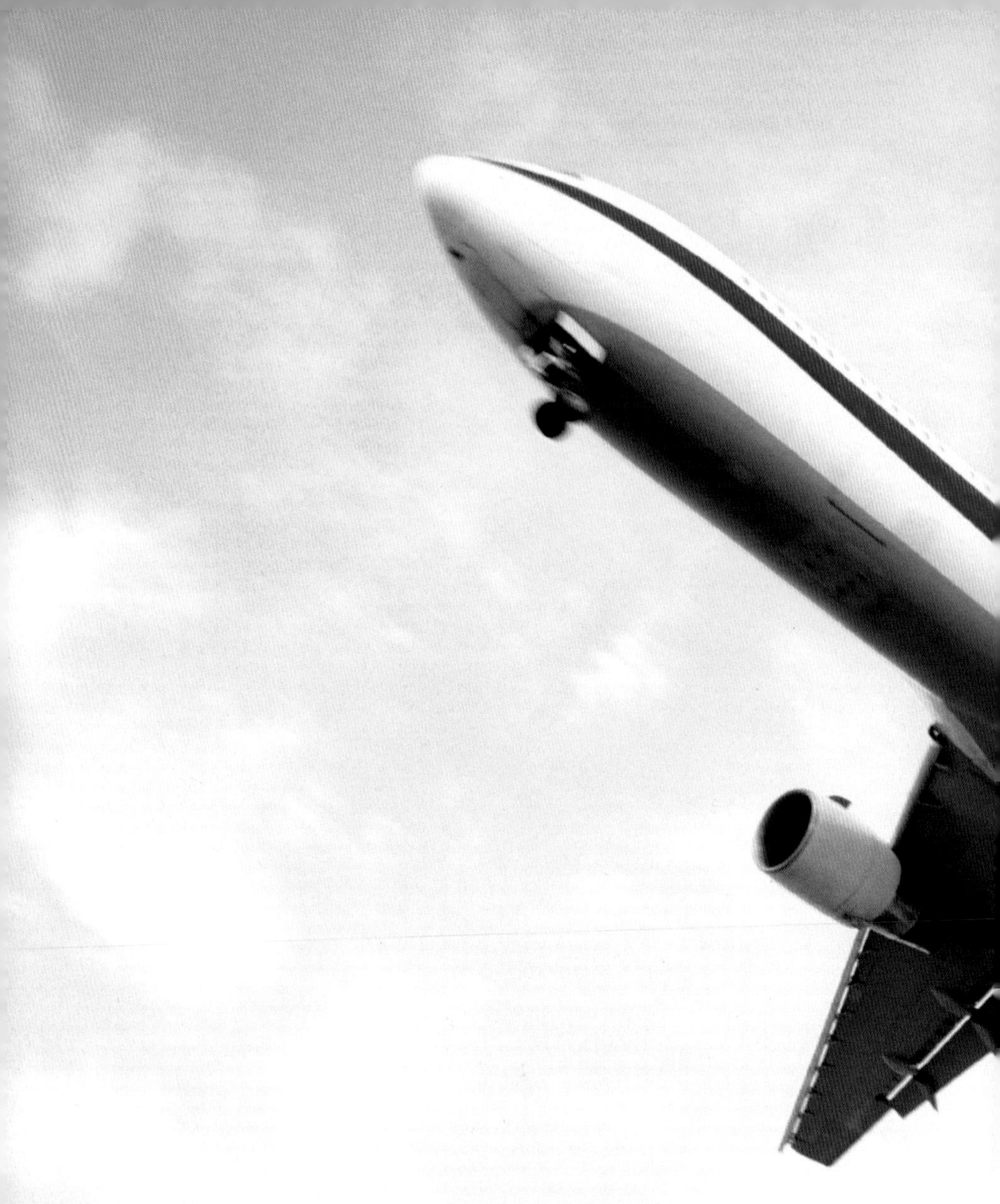

P is for plane.

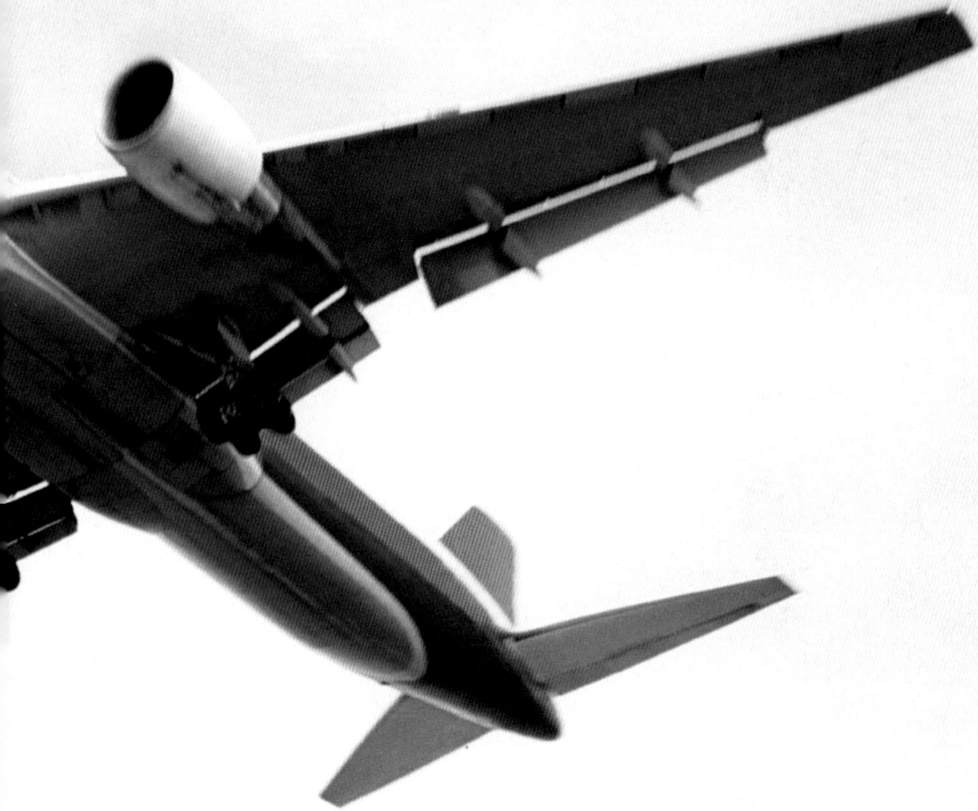

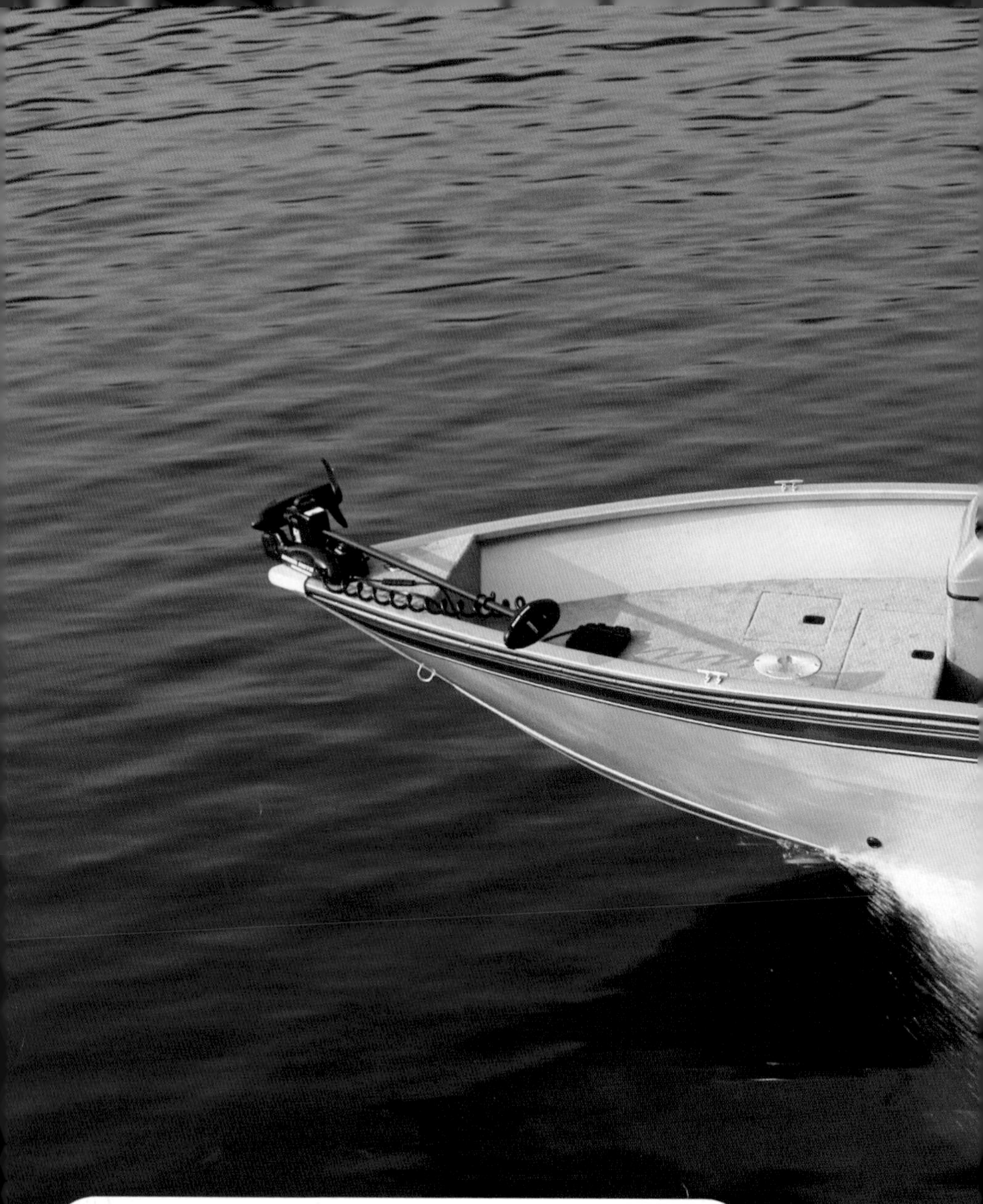

B is for boat.

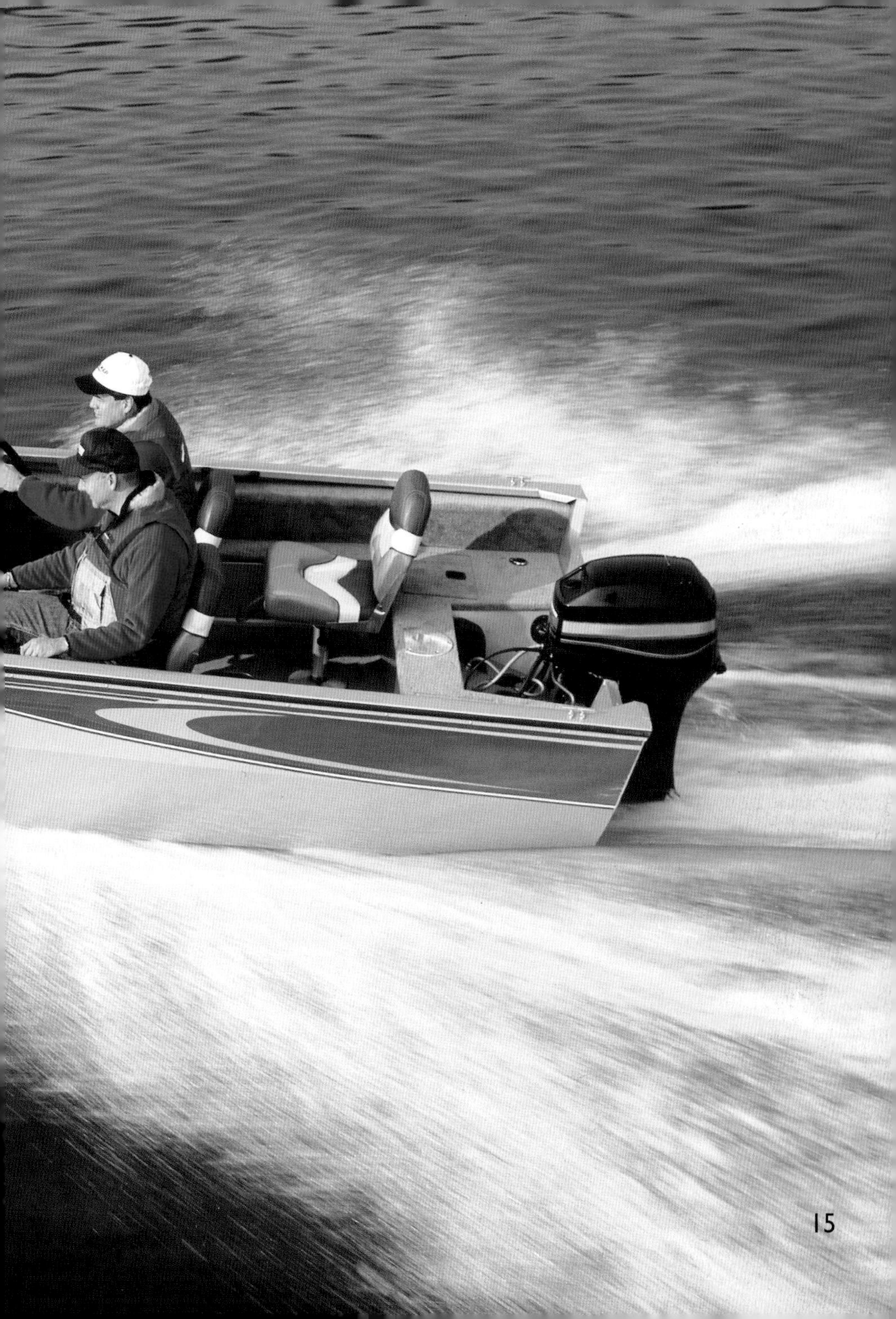

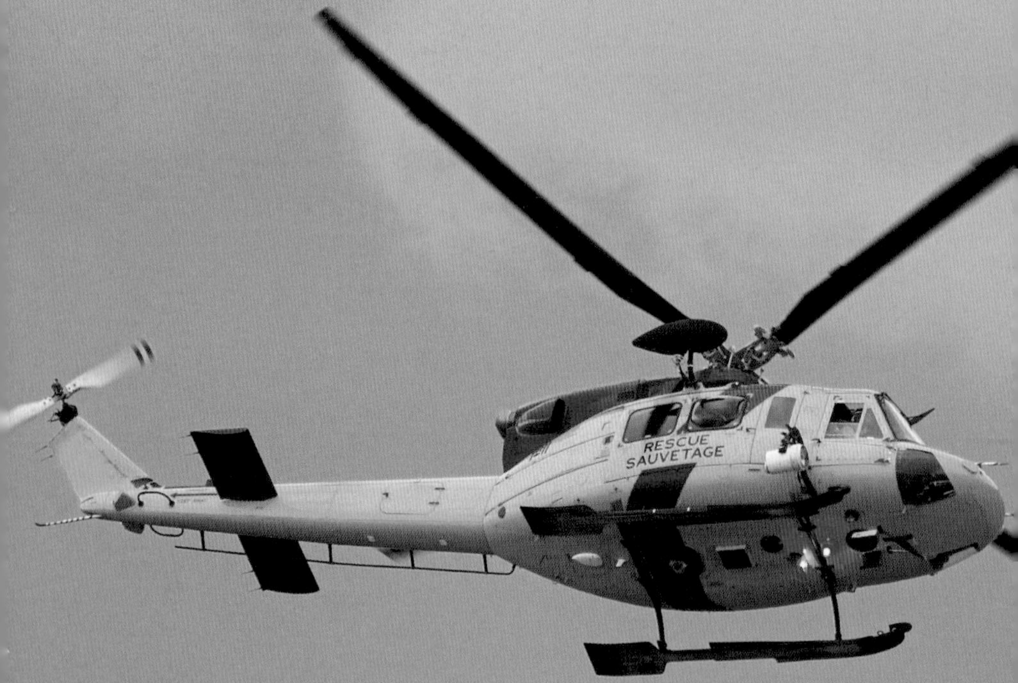

H is for helicopter.